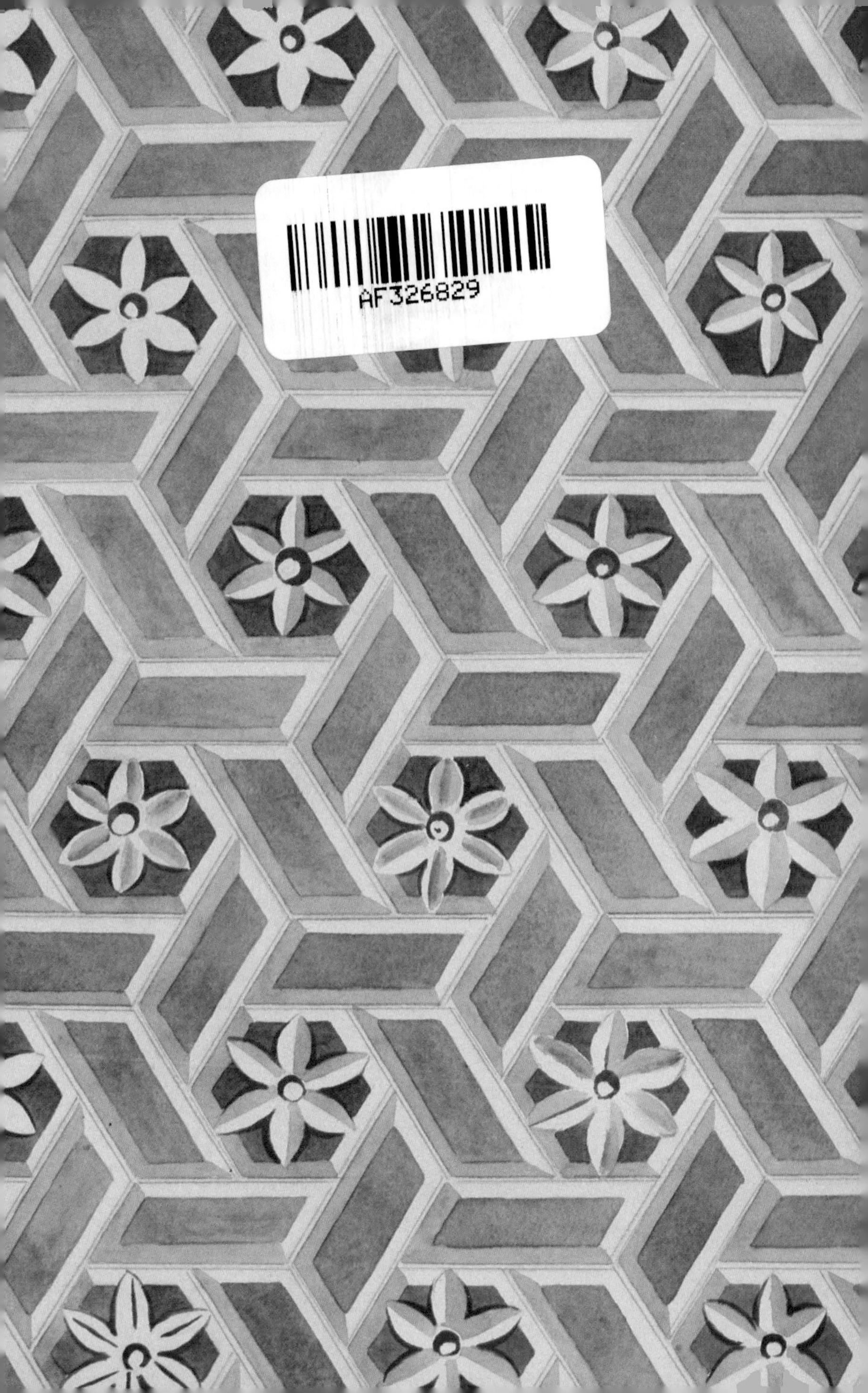
AF326829

THE VICTORIA AND ALBERT COLOUR BOOKS

LIBRARY OF CONGRESS CATALOGING-IN-PUBLICATION DATA

STRONGE, SUSAN.
INDIAN ARCHITECTURAL DESIGNS / TEXT BY SUSAN STRONGE.
P. CM. - (THE VICTORIA AND ALBERT COLOUR BOOKS)
BIBLIOGRAPHY: P.
ISBN 0-8109-3905-3

1. ARCHITECTURE - INDIA - FATIHPUR SIKRI - DETAILS. 2. ARCHITECTURE - INDIA - AGRA (DISTRICT) - DETAILS. 3. ARCHITECTURE, MOGUL - INDIA - FATIHPUR SIKRI - THEMES, MOTIVES 4. ARCHITECTURE, MOGUL - INDIA - AGRA (DISTRICT) - THEMES, MOTIVES. 5. ARCHITECTURE, ISLAMIC - INDIA - FATIHPUR SIKRI - THEMES, MOTIVES. 6. ARCHITECTURE, ISLAMIC - INDIA - AGRA (DISTRICT) - THEMES, MOTIVES. 7. FATIHPUR SIKRI (INDIA) - BUILDINGS, STRUCTURES, ETC. 8. VICTORIA AND ALBERT MUSEUM. INDIAN SECTION. I. TITLE. II. SERIES.
NA2840.S75 1989
722'.44'2 - DC 19   88 - 35708

INDIAN ARCHITECTURAL DESIGNS

INTRODUCTION BY
SUSAN STRONGE

HARRY N. ABRAMS, INC., PUBLISHERS
NEW YORK

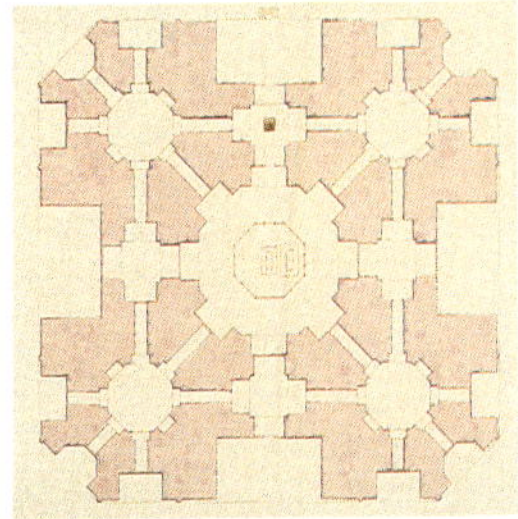

IN 1880, Caspar Purdon Clarke of the South Kensington Museum was sent to India to buy contemporary art manufactures which would remedy the supposed deficiencies of the Indian collections. The purpose of these acquisitions was twofold: it was hoped both to encourage craft industries in India by stimulating demand and to acquire artefacts which 'by perfection of design or ornamentation' would have an improving effect on British manufactures.

Purdon Clarke left London in the guise of a Second Secretary in the Diplomatic Service, a uniform of some description being deemed necessary to mark his official position as the Museum's representative. He returned two years later, having shipped back no less than 3421 items. Amongst the expected contemporary jewellery, pottery, textiles and metalwork was a huge range of architectural material including plaster casts of intact buildings, sections of ruined monuments, modern copies of eighteenth-century tiled façades, and a series of water-colour drawings entitled 'Rubbings from stone carvings, Agra district'.

A few of the drawings are inscribed with the name of the building from which the detail was taken, several give the precise location of the detail on the buildings, while omitting the name of the building itself, but most are uninscribed. Neither the circumstances of their acquisition, nor information about who made the drawings from the rubbings, have survived in museum records. It is, however, clear that most show details from monuments erected for, or in the time of, the Mughal emperor Jalal ad-Din Muhammad Akbar

(1556-1605). The exceptions found so far are those details taken from the tomb of I'timad ad-Daula, which dates from 1628.

Most of the drawings are of details found on the structures of an extraordinary city founded by Akbar in 1571 at Sikri, twenty-four miles west of Agra. Sikri was the residence of Shaikh Salim ad-Din Chishti, a member of a Sufi order which had arrived in India in the twelfth century. The shaikh had prophesied that Akbar would have three sons, at a time when all his other offspring had died in infancy. Shortly afterwards, in 1569, Akbar's wife gave birth to his first son at Sikri. A second son was also born at Sikri the following year and Akbar decided to commemorate these events by building a new city there.

The city was named Fathabad, 'City of Victory', which eventually became anglicized as Fatehpur-Sikri. The pace of construction was rapid: work on the palace complex began in 1571 and its main building was completed in 1576; a huge mosque was finished in 1575 or 1576; the bazaar and market-place were commissioned in 984 AH/AD 1576-77. Within a remarkably short space of time, a city had appeared almost out of nothing on the sandstone ridge overlooking a lake. It became a bustling commercial centre and imperial ateliers were moved there to produce paintings and luxury artefacts for the court. An English visitor to the city in 1584 described it as being 'greater than London and very populous'.

In 1585 Akbar left Fatehpur-Sikri for Lahore and, though returning for short visits, never again lived in it. The life of the city ebbed away and as early as 1615 a second English visitor commented that it had 'gone much to decaye and is nowe verye ruinous'. Today a great deal of the city remains, though the lake has become a dry plain. Despite many references to specific, named buildings in contemporary histories, few of these can be identified with the existing structures. The sometimes quaint and often misleading names now used for them seem to have been made up by a local guide in the nineteenth century and were given wide currency by Edmund Smith, who produced a four-volume survey of the site between 1895 and 1898. These are also the names given, in slightly garbled form, in the Purdon Clarke drawings.

The monuments of Fatehpur-Sikri reveal major stylistic influences. They use, as other Indian monuments for Muslim patrons had before them, the indigenous trabeate methods of construction. Their style depends heavily on the Muslim buildings of Gujarat which had, in their turn, absorbed western Indian Hindu and Jain architectural styles. The wooden structures of Central Asia inspired the carved surfaces on some of the buildings, which are simply wood-carvings rendered in the local mottled pink sandstone. Iran is a major source of decorative motifs and Iranian tile forms of much earlier date may be seen echoed in one of the patterns taken from a *jali,* or pierced screen (*plate 22*).

The surface ornamentation in Fatehpur-Sikri ranges from the purely geometric to the purely naturalistic, but it is interesting to note that Purdon Clarke has concentrated on the immensely complicated geometrical designs, or on the extremely formalized floral arabesque or scrolling patterns, excluding motifs such as the more realistic flowering plants, trees and animals that are also to be found. One of the most delicately rendered scrolls in the series, the pomegranate panel from the Turkish Sultana's House (*plate 4*) stands out because of its relative freeness of execution.

This characteristic is also true of the details taken from the much later tomb of I'timad ad-Daula (*plate 12*); the patterns inlaid into the white marble walls of vases within cusped arches have been ignored in favour of the beautiful, flowing rhythms of the scrolling ornament on the floor, bordered by a starkly contrasting row of isolated rosettes.

The endlessly fascinating geometrical patterns, their internal logic so confusing to the Western viewer not accustomed to it, were those which clearly fascinated Purdon Clarke most: the details taken from Akbar's mausoleum at Sikandra (*plates 16, 7 and 23*) display the same concern for mathematically determined ornament. A detail from a pierced screen, or a relief panel, shows squares arranged along two intersecting axes (*plate 15*), an effect which constantly draws the eye in opposing directions. The difficulty of copying these, even from a rubbing, is indicated by the fact that, unlike the original, few of the squares are true.

Other patterns are relatively simple, such as those of squares within octagons on the same sheet, or the stars within hexagons or squares (*plate 21*), but attract close attention by the interlocking of the elements of the pattern which set up different rhythms depending on which structures within it are selected.

The other sheets in the series of drawings show flowers and half-palmettes, of key importance in the development of Mughal architectural design. Some are more purely geometrical, but have flowers or rosettes inserted into the overall plan (*plates 18, 13 and 2*), and set into their own separate spaces. Other patterns relate to carpet design or to manuscript illustration and the flowers or leaves are integral, rather than dominant, parts of the overall plan (*panel, plate 10*).

In certain designs which seem to be specific to Fatehpur-Sikri and the contemporary buildings at Agra and nearby, the vegetal elements are given more prominence (*plates 19, 2, 4 and 20*), even though transformed by the stonemasons from reasonably simple leaf forms into extremely bizarre flights of fancy.

This may also be seen in the details from two column bases (*plate 5*). On the left, the half-lotus rosette is an indigenous motif; the frame derives from Buddhist architectural forms. The arabesque designs above the lotus come from an Iranian repertoire of ornament which could have been easily adapted to the surfaces of metalwork or on to manuscripts and carpets, though the curling, serrated leaves are exaggeratedly attenuated by Iranian standards. On the right, the arabesque has been thrust aside by an enormous palmette with a few leaf tendrils squeezed around it, and contained within a lobed and cusped arch.

This sprouting vegetation paves the way for the predominantly floral architectural decoration of the reign of Shah Jahan (1628-58) when some of India's most famous monuments were produced. The drawings therefore seem to reflect a dual interest: the development of the Mughal style, and a fascination with ornament of a kind that could not, because of its complexity, be easily copied in the West.

A consideration of the man who collected the drawings offers an explanation for these choices, whilst shedding light on a particular phase in the development of British architectural ideas.

Purdon Clarke was an architect by profession, trained at the South Kensington Art Schools, and in many ways was ideally suited to his task. During his early career he had been in charge of the building of the British Consulate in Tehran. He had been sent on purchasing trips for the South Kensington Museum to Turkey and Syria as well as Europe, and was the architect of the Indian pavilion at the 1878 Paris exhibition. Following the transfer of the Indian Museum's collections to South Kensington in 1880, he arranged them in their new home and must have been closely involved in the preparation of Sir George Birdwood's handbook to the collection, *The Industrial Arts of India*. Written, rather unconventionally, as a guide to the defects of the collection rather than as a description of what was actually in it, Purdon Clarke had only to follow the book chapter by chapter to execute his mission successfully.

The acquisition of drawings of architectural details was the result of the growing awareness of Indian arts and crafts that had begun with the Great Exhibition in London in 1851. The leading critics of the day (notably Owen Jones in his *Grammar of Ornament*) had deplored the standard of design in the Western manufactures on show both in 1851 and in the Paris exhibition of 1862, comparing them unfavourably with the freshness and vigour of contemporary Indian products. 'Saracenic' decoration was also greatly praised by Jones. The ideas which, in Britain, swelled into the Arts and Crafts movement, produced an examination of Western interaction with artistic production, in its widest sense, in India. Many were aware that the crafts were in serious decline in the West, and were equally aware that the art schools that had been set up to remedy the situation were actually contributing to it.

In a lecture given to the Royal Society of Arts in 1890, Purdon Clarke drew attention to the architecture that was being produced by the British in India – the 'monuments of shame', as he put it. He commented that 'After running the gamut of the styles in Greek, Strawberry Hill Gothic, and representations of the several periods of Pointed architecture in colleges and churches, we eventually woke up to the fact that India had a style more suited to the country than any of those we had tried to introduce.' Having woken up to this, architects with no experience in, or knowledge of, Eastern design were suddenly ordered to erect important buildings acknowledging local forms and styles. He concluded that, though more appropriate than earlier efforts, they would long remain a record of British lack of appreciation of 'the essentials of Eastern Art'. If the Western architect was to effect a successful synthesis of Indian elements into his plans, access to a portfolio of Indian architectural details was an absolute necessity.

By 1880, reliable information on Indian architecture was becoming available in a way impossible before the 1850s. Photography had a major impact and was widely disseminated through the international exhibitions. The first books on Indian architecture also appeared and the creation of the Archaeological Survey of India in 1870 inaugurated a steady stream of important architectural studies.

There was thus a certain amount of reference material available, but as an architect producing, albeit on a very small scale, buildings of the kind he was advocating for India, Clarke must have been acutely aware of the need for studies which could have a much more practical application. Collecting his own material was a short-term solution. The growing demand for material of this nature is confirmed by the appearance, in 1890, of the six-volume *Jeypore Portfolio* by Colonel Samuel Swinton Jacob. It contained details of buildings in Delhi, Agra and Rajasthan 'in such a shape as to be of practical use to the architect and artizan'.

The result of all these efforts was the emergence of a new architectural style which Raymond Head calls 'Imperial Anglo-Indian'. In its use of authentic detail it was exactly what was being advocated by Purdon Clarke. Its creators were architects like Major Charles Mant, Robert Chisholm, Colonel S S Jacob and F S Growse, who were clearly those being praised, though not by name, in a lecture given by Purdon Clarke in 1888 to the

Royal Institute of British Architects. Head points out that when Mant had needed details of Indian buildings for his own work, he had been forced to visit the key monuments in India himself, to take photographs and make detailed drawings. The style could not have developed without the increase in the number of studies on Indian architecture: the Purdon Clarke drawings are documents which mark a small, but important, stage in the process.

FURTHER READING

E. W. Smith *The Moghul Architecture of Fatehpur-Sikri*, 4 vols., Allahabad: Archaeological Survey of India, 1894-98.

Michael Brand and Glenn D. Lowry (eds) *Fatehpur-Sikri. A Sourcebook*, The Aga Khan Program for Islamic Architecture, Cambridge, Massachusetts, 1985.

Michael Brand and Glenn D. Lowry *Fatehpur-Sikri*, Marg Publications, Bombay, 1986 (see especially Ebba Koch "The Architectural Forms", pp 121-48).

Raymond Head *The Indian Style*, London, 1986.

THE PLATES

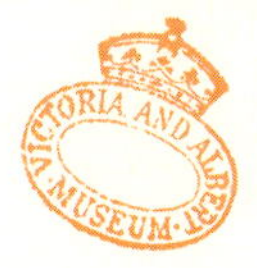

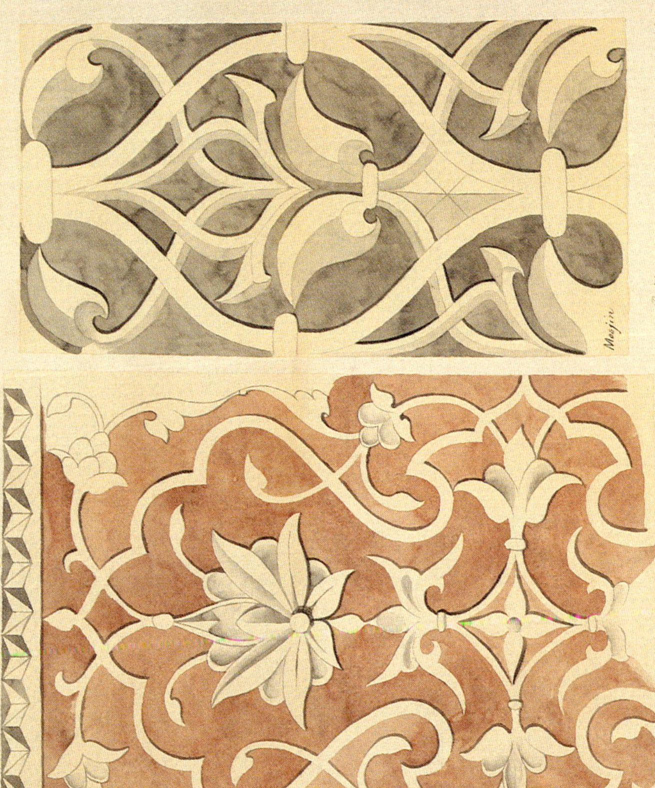

Masjid
Rubbings from stone carvings, Agra District. 1882 & 1883.15
Panel in centre of wall below Niche N.W. Room Birbul's Daughter's E. Side.

Fathahpoor Dargah

Panel of marble Bath Room

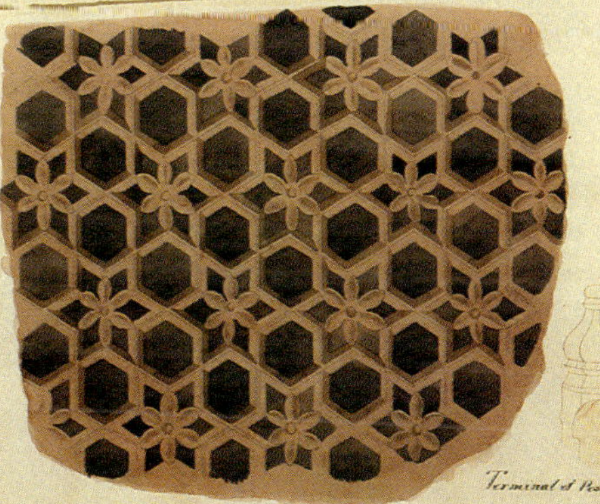

Terminal of Post between railing panels.

Rubbings from Stone carvings, Agra District.

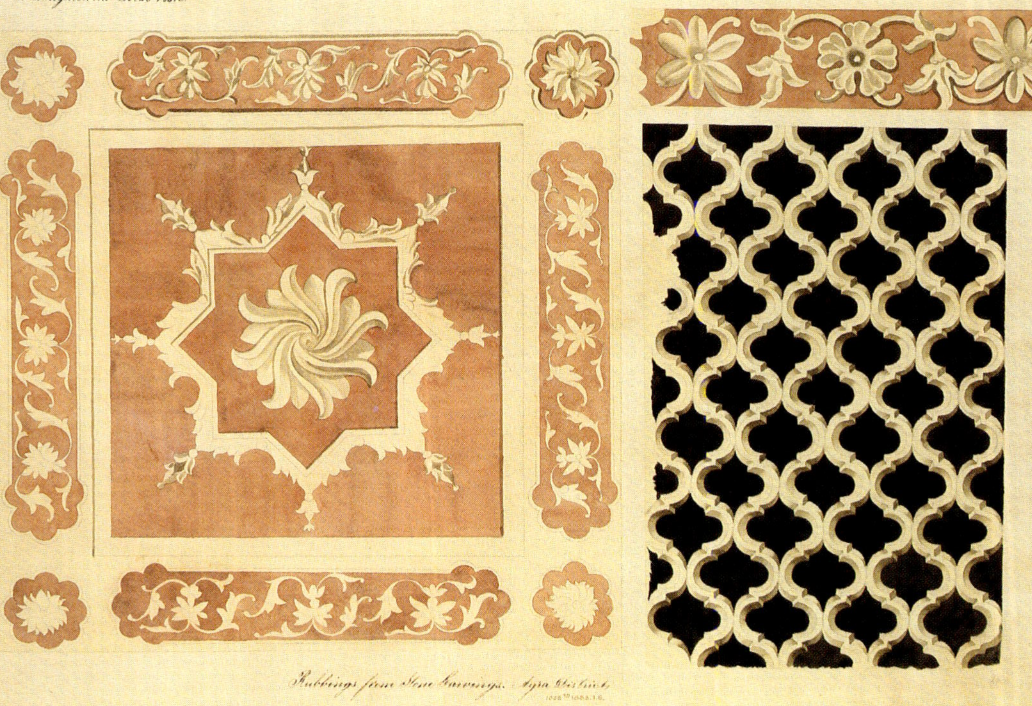

3

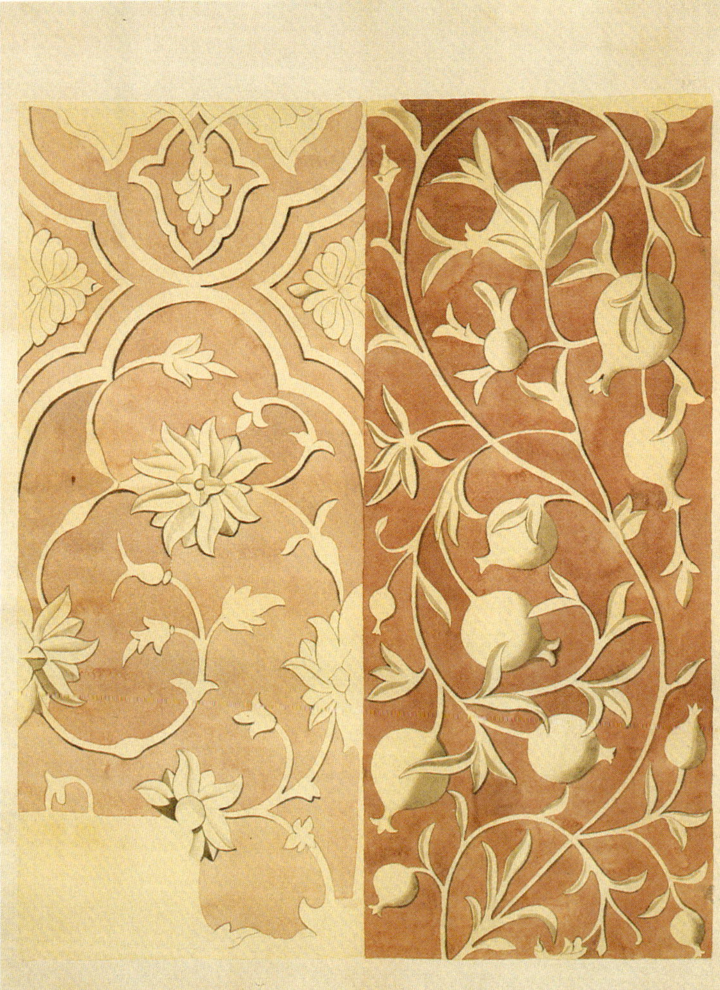

Rubbings from stone carvings, Agra District

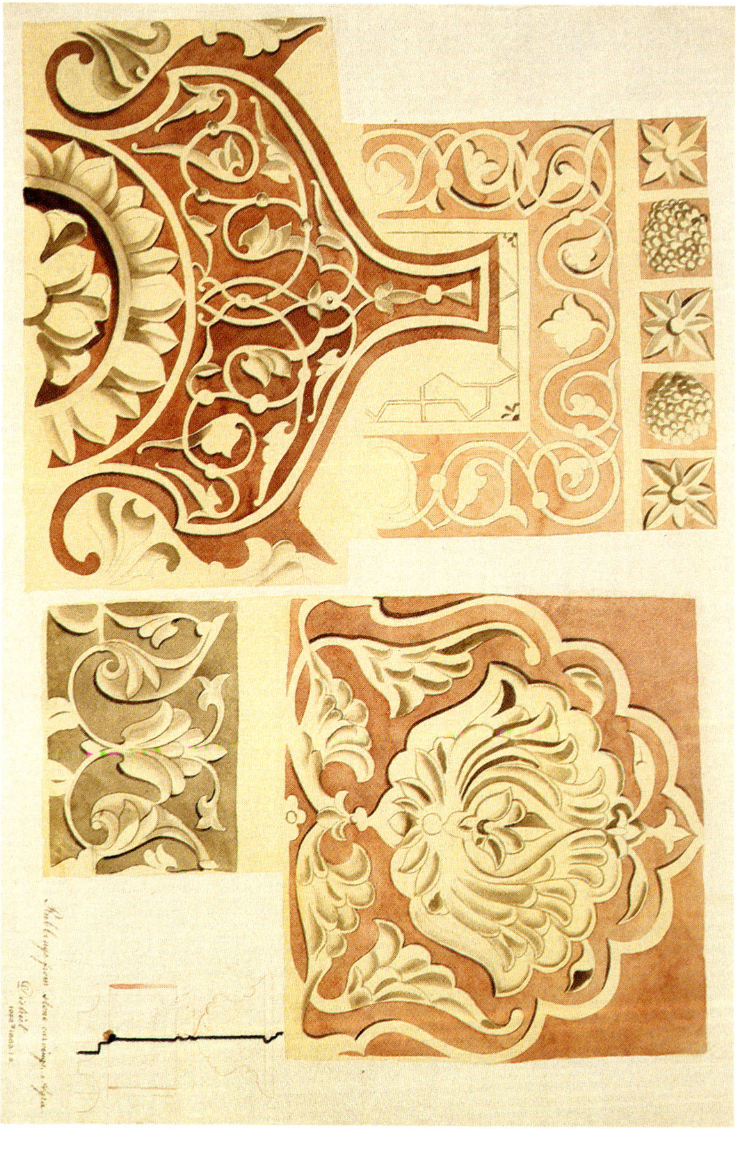

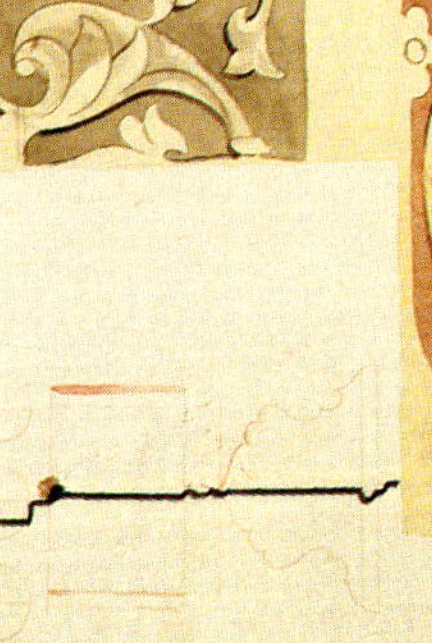

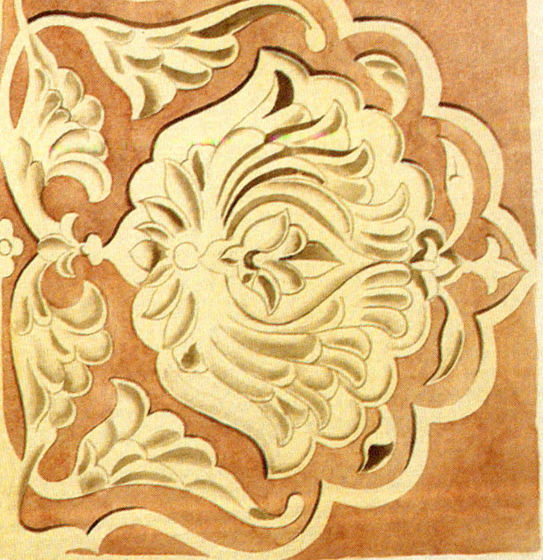

Dewan-i-Khas.
Upper base of Pillar

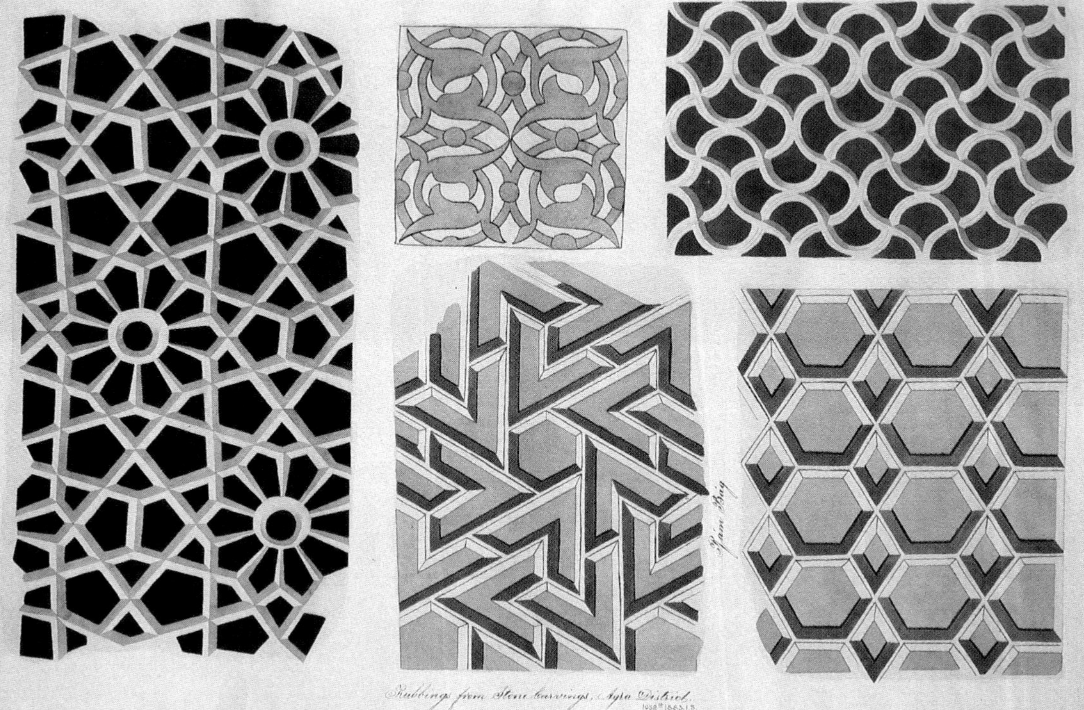
Rubbings from Stone Carvings, Agra District.
Jam Bág

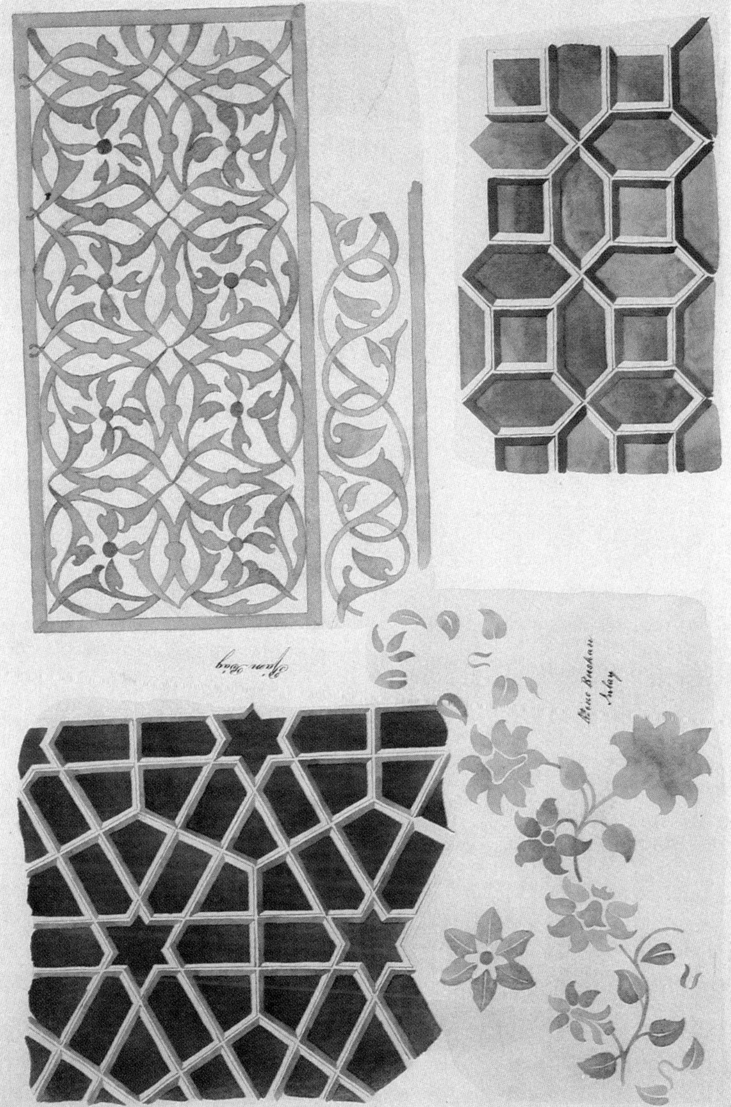

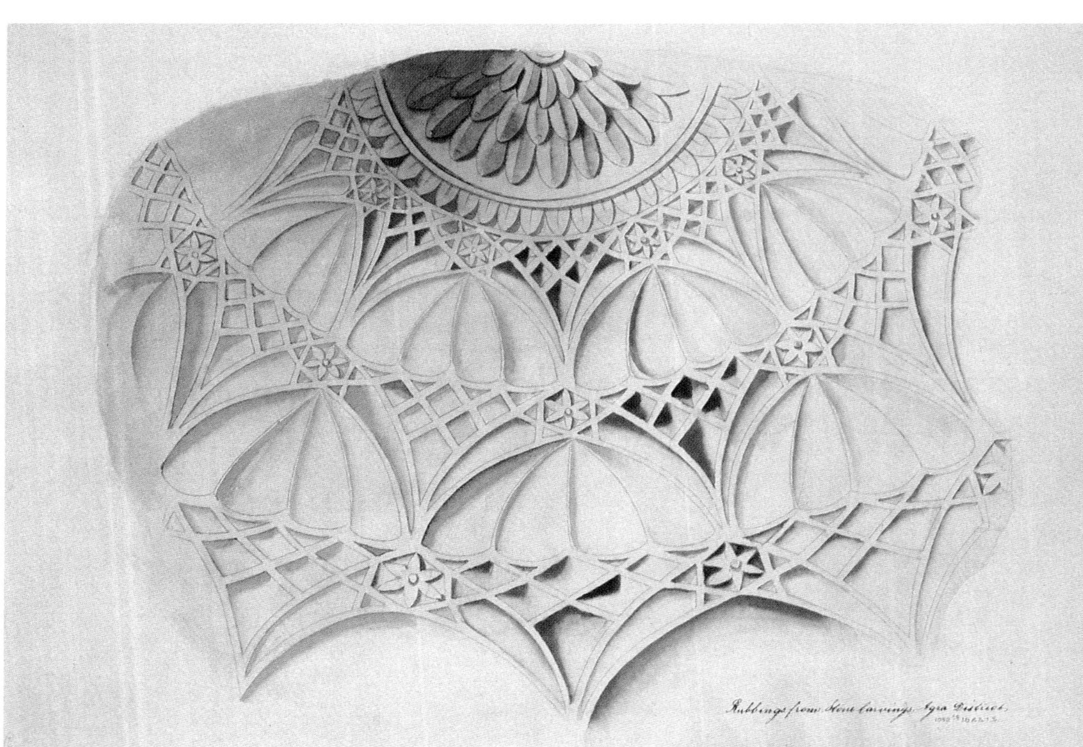
Rubbings from Stone Carvings. Agra District.

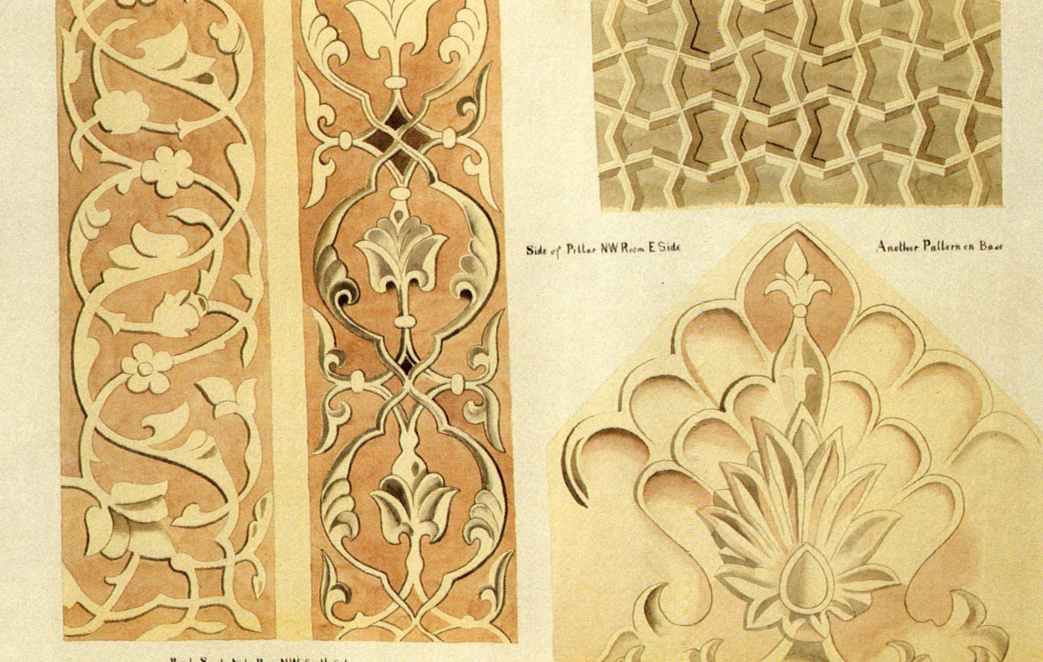

Rubbings from stone Carvings, Agra District

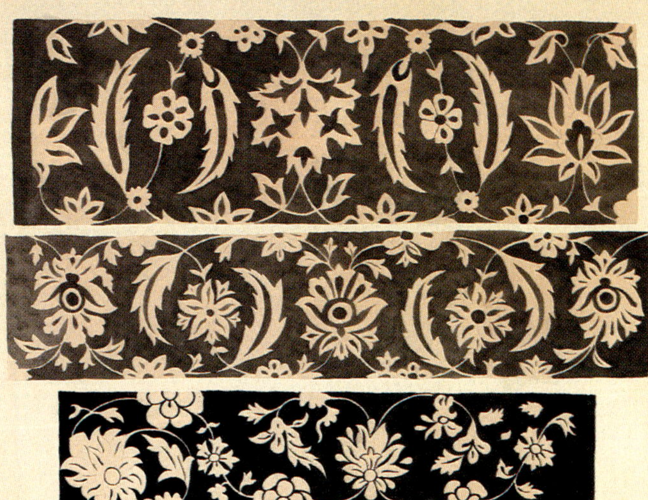

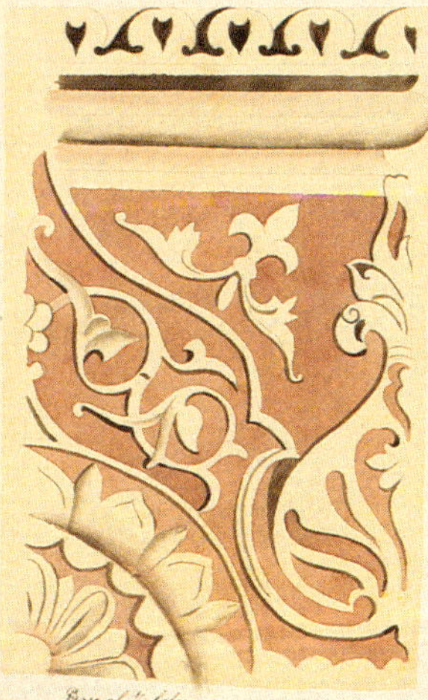

Base of a Column

Rubbings from Stone Carvings, Agra District.

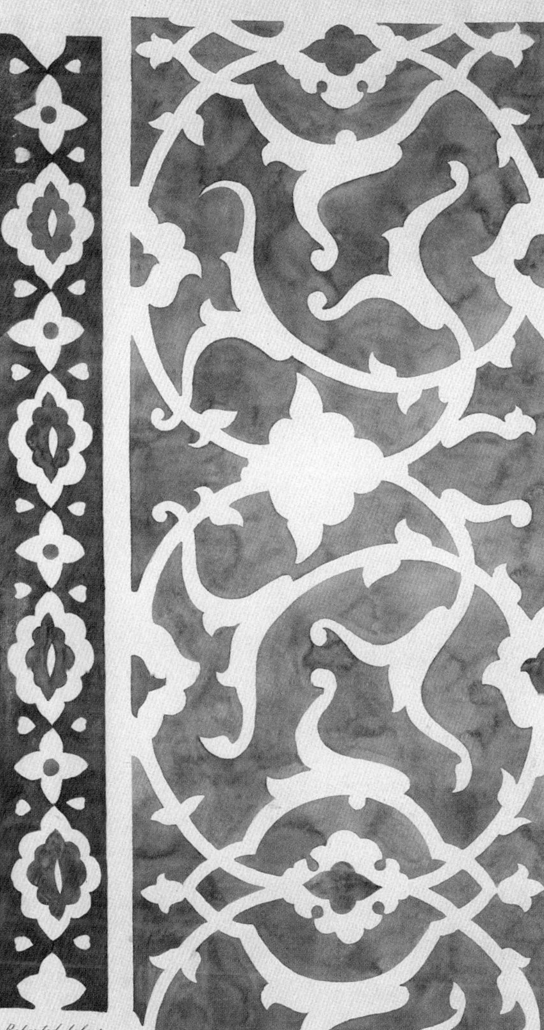
Rubbings from Stone Carvings, Agra District
Repeated below.

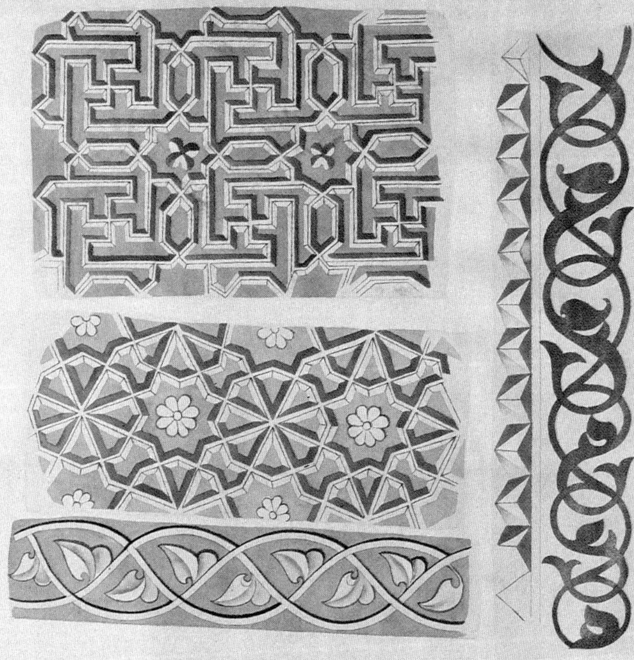

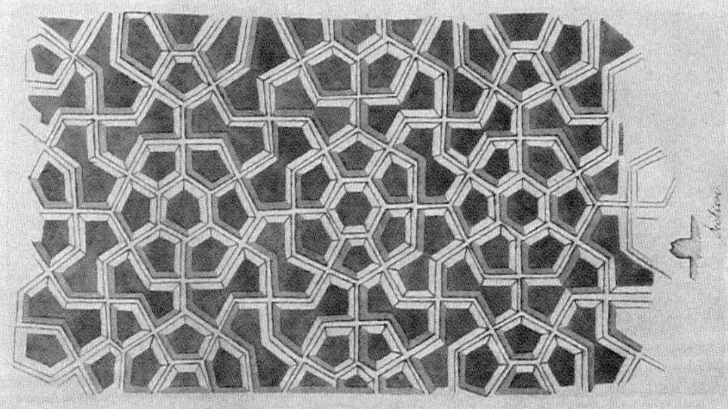

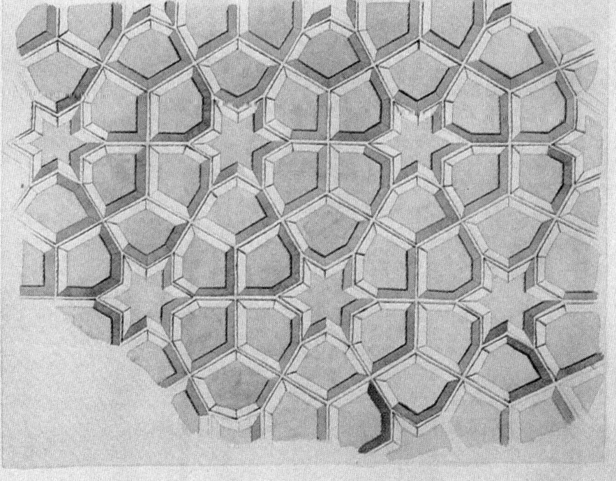

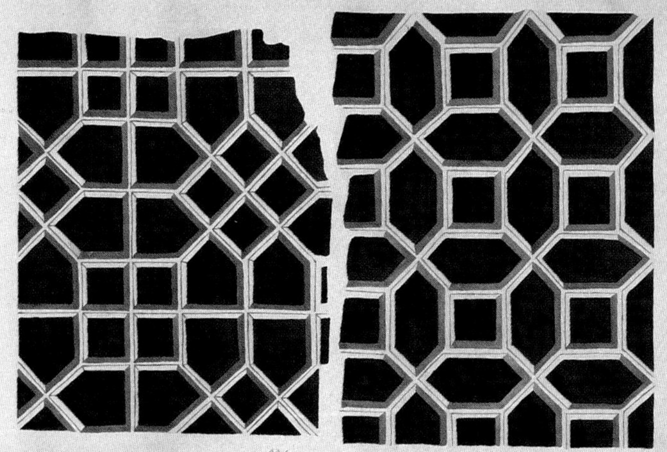

Ram Bag.

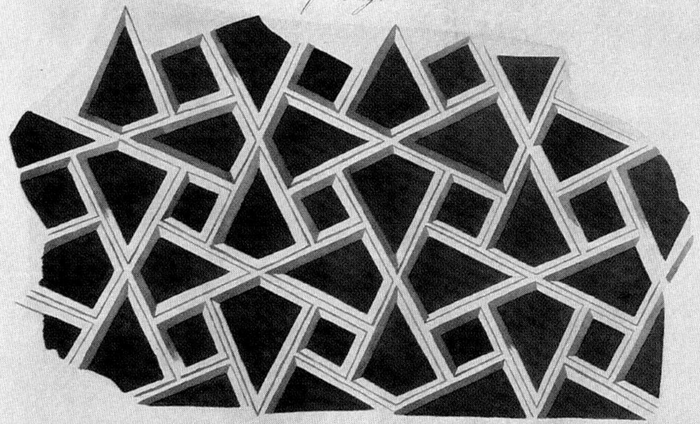

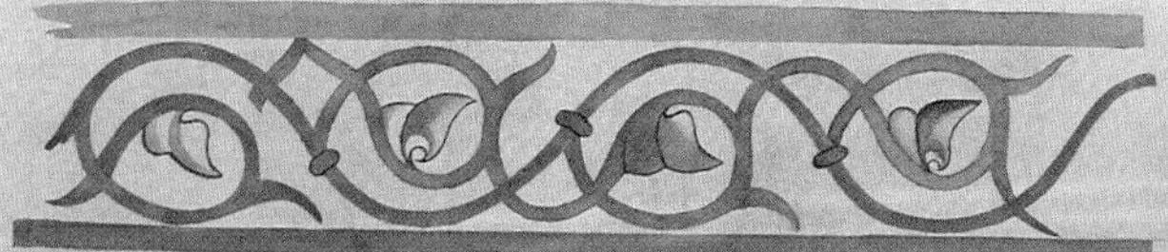

Rubbings from Stone Carvings, Agra District.   The dark parts raised.

Section

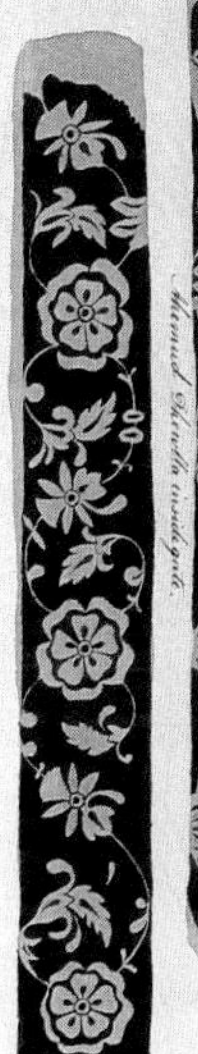

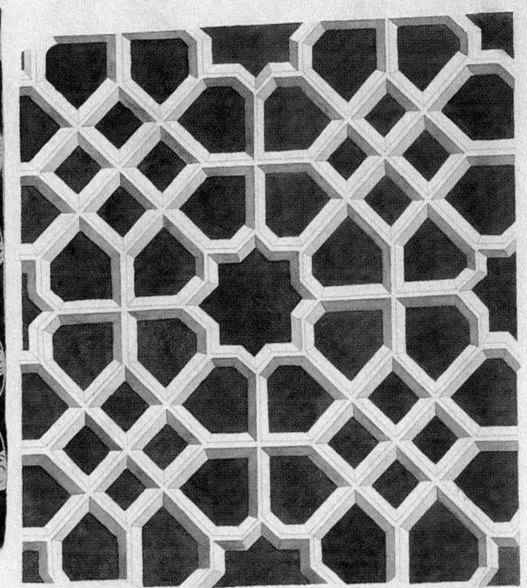

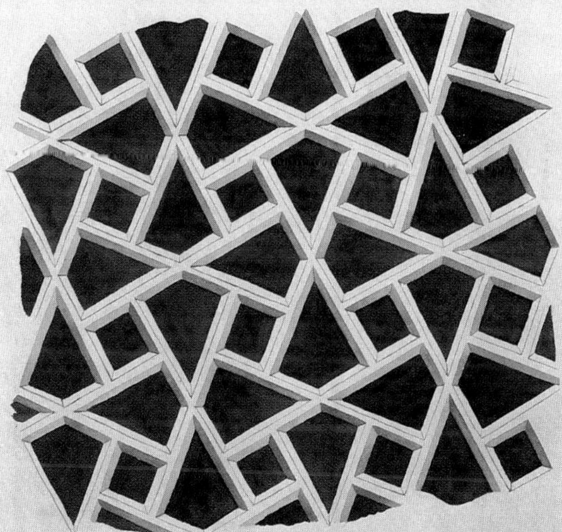

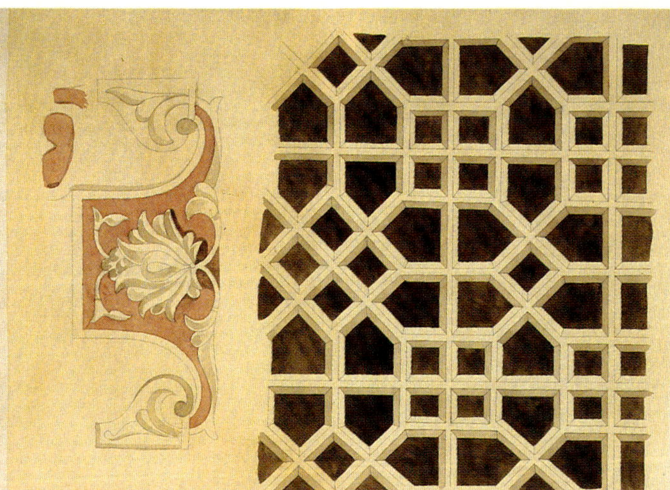

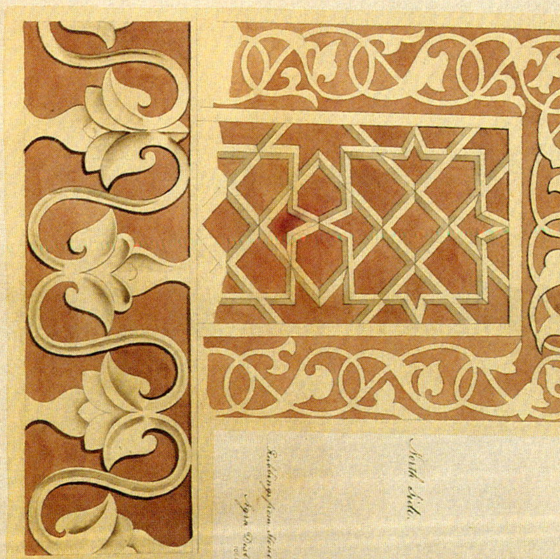

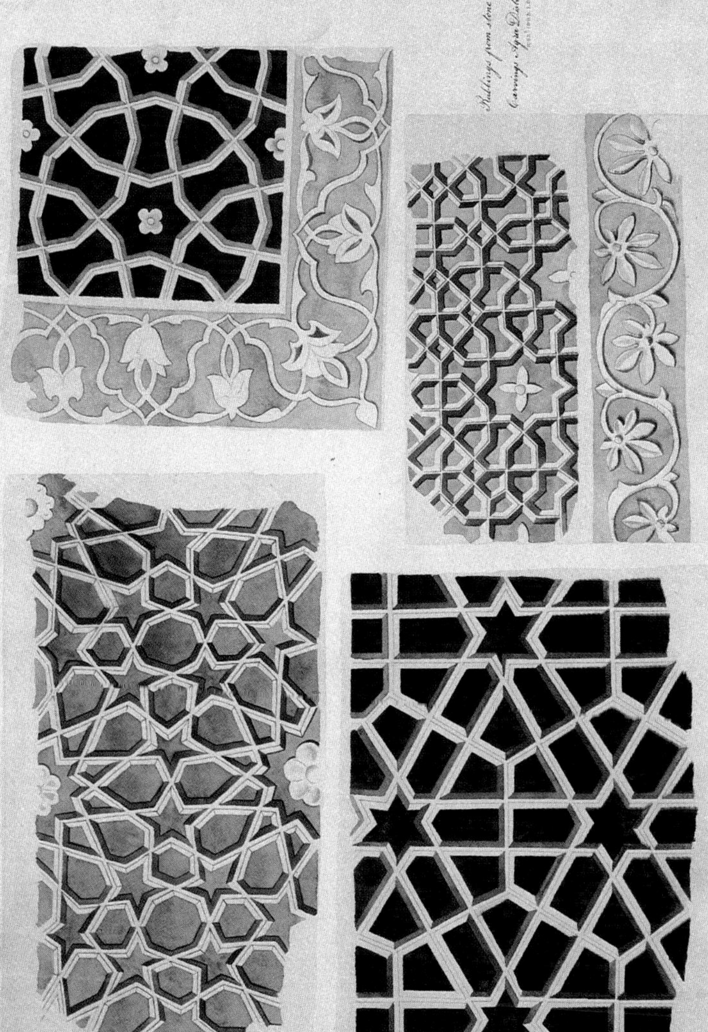
Rubbings from stone
carvings Agra Delhi

Rubbings from Stone Carvings, Agra District.
1052.53.I.S.

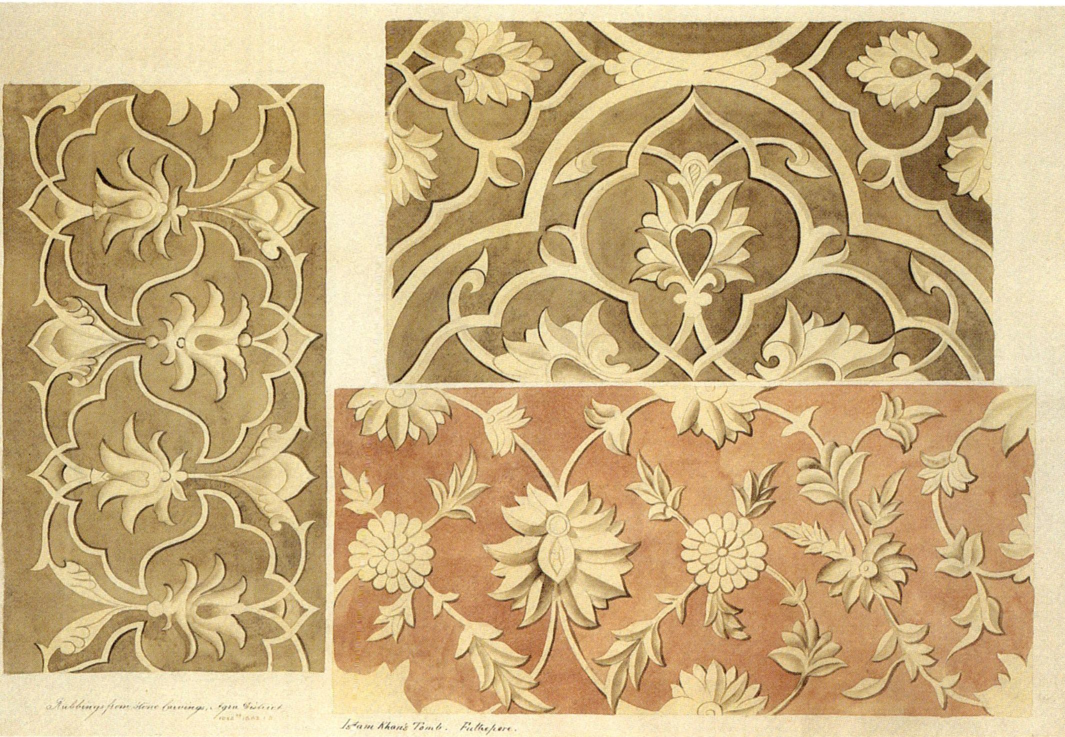

Rubbings from Stone Carvings, Agra District.

Islam Khan's Tomb. Futtehpore.

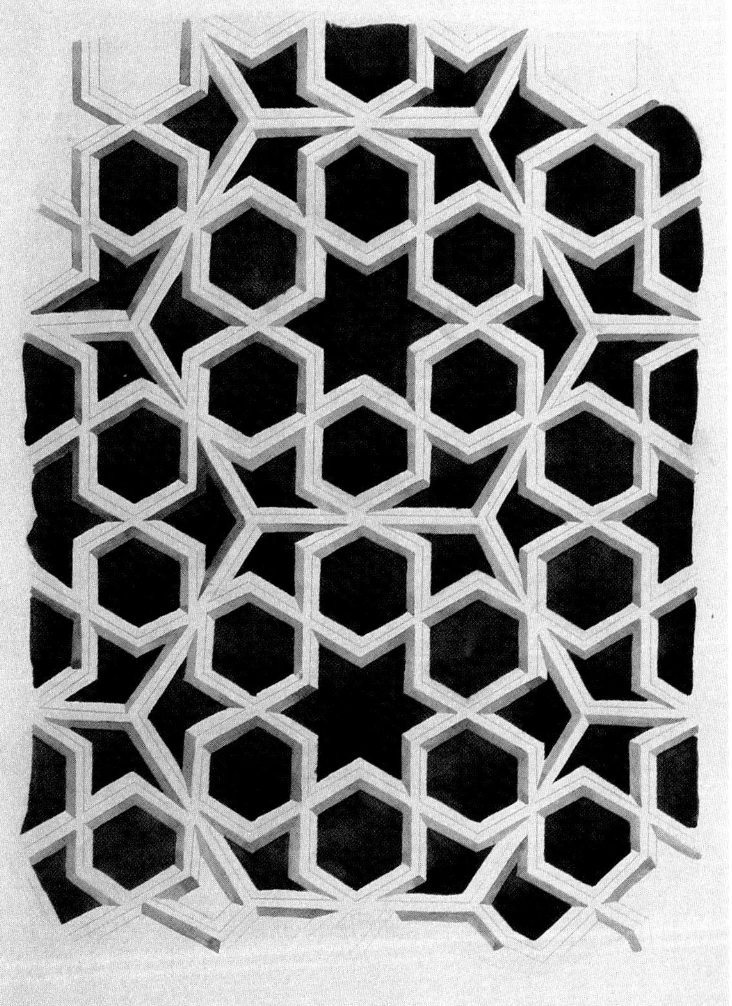

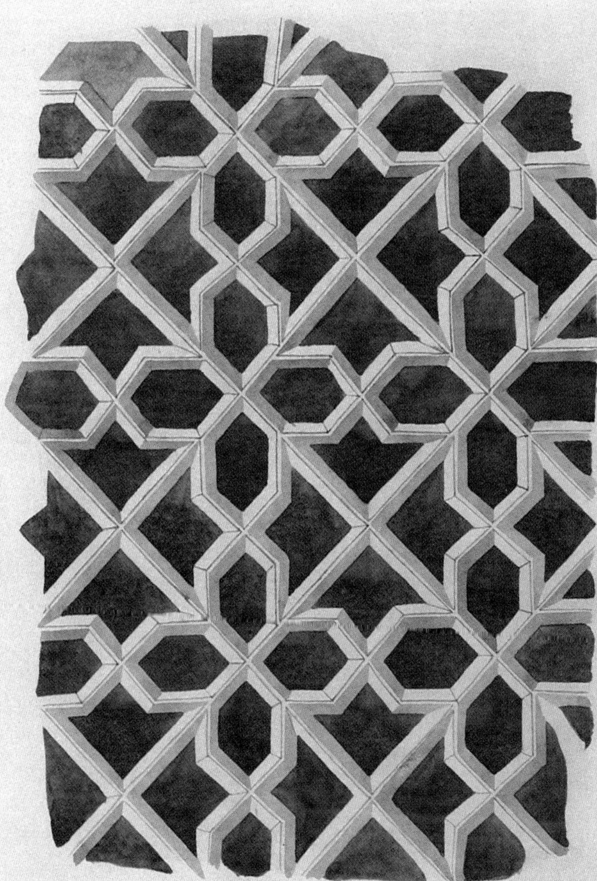

Rubbins from Stone Carvings, Agra District
1032^d 1883. I.S.

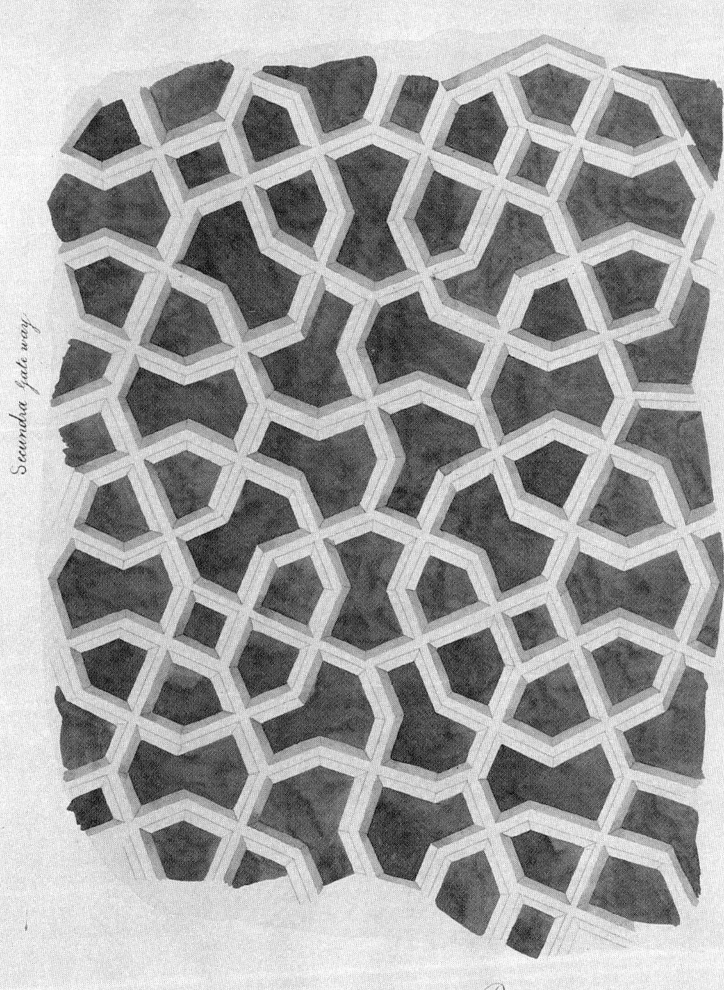

Secundra gate way

Rubbings from stone carvings

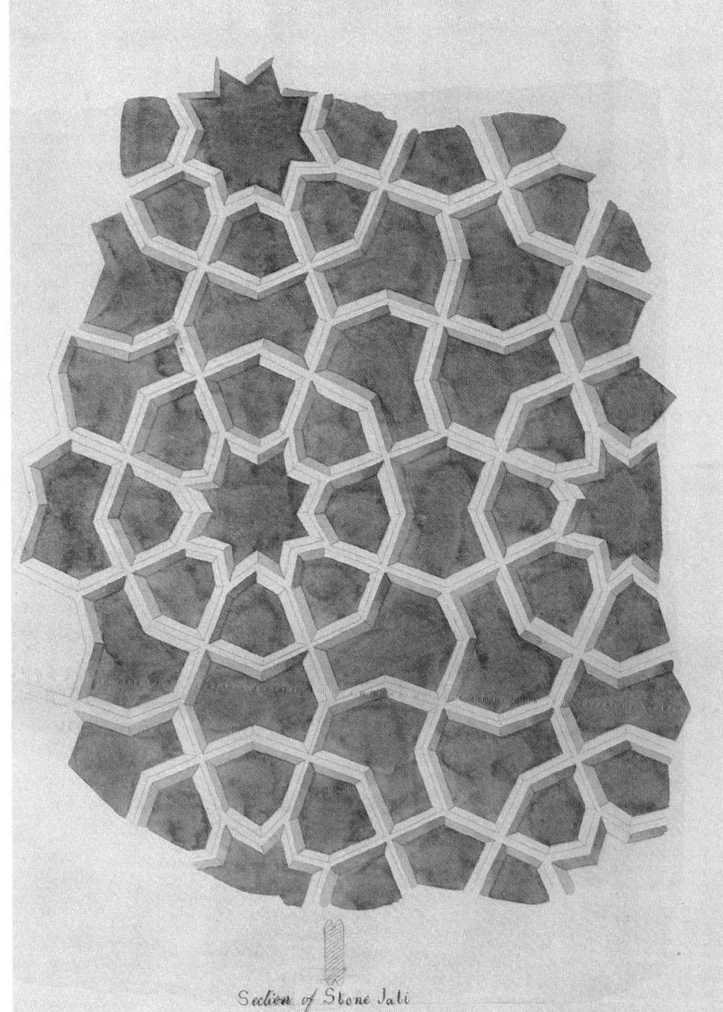

Section of Stone Jali

Agra District
1052ᴱ 1883.I.S.

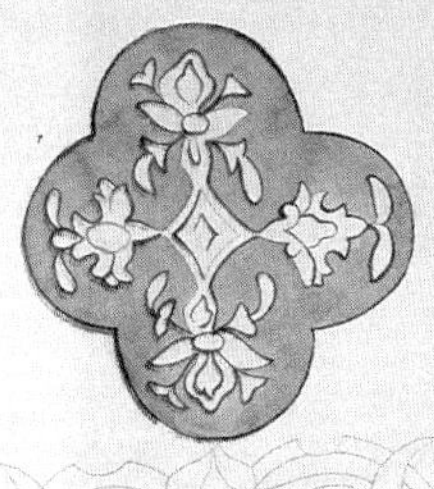

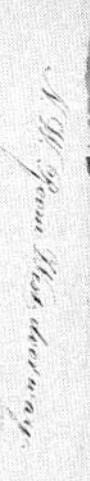

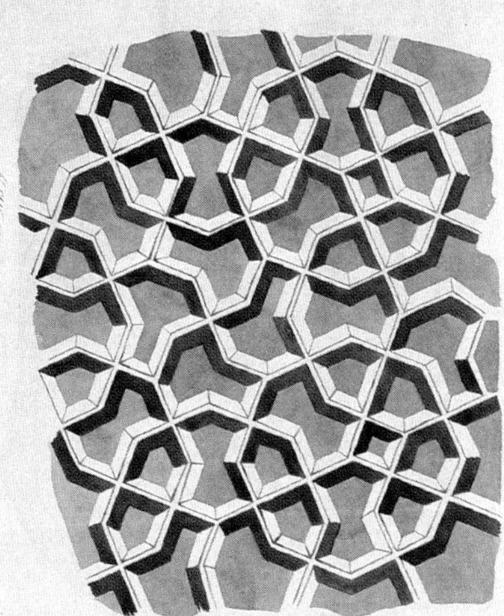

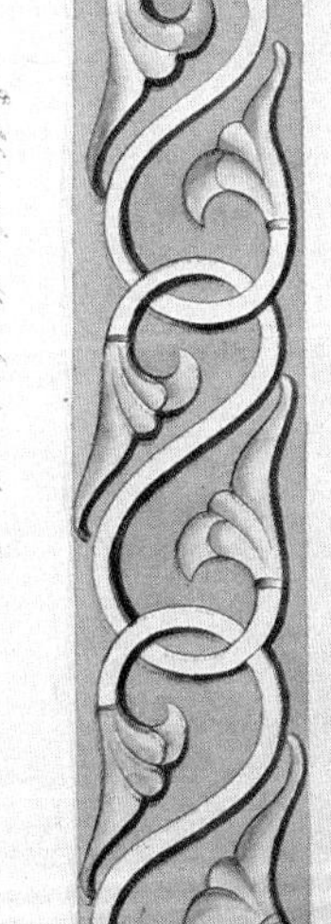

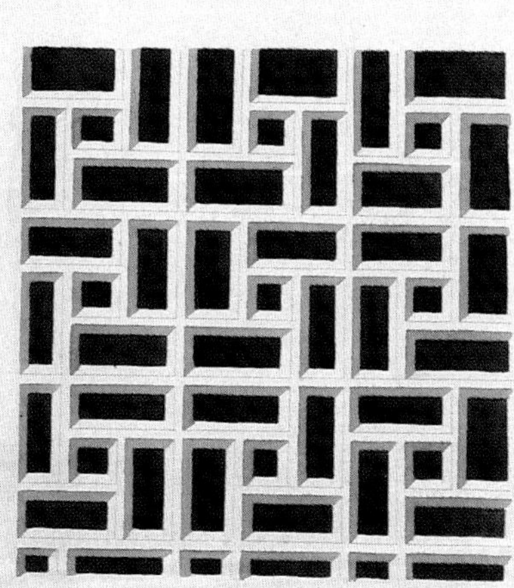

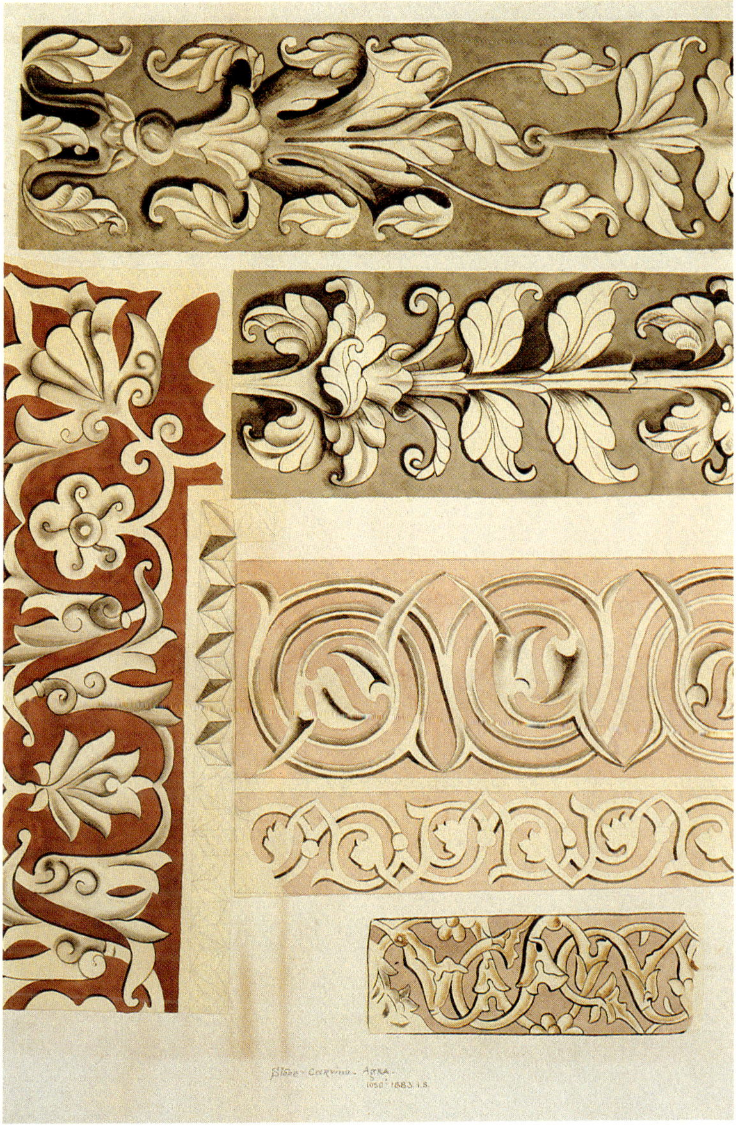

STONE CARVING - AGRA.
1050? 1883. I.S.

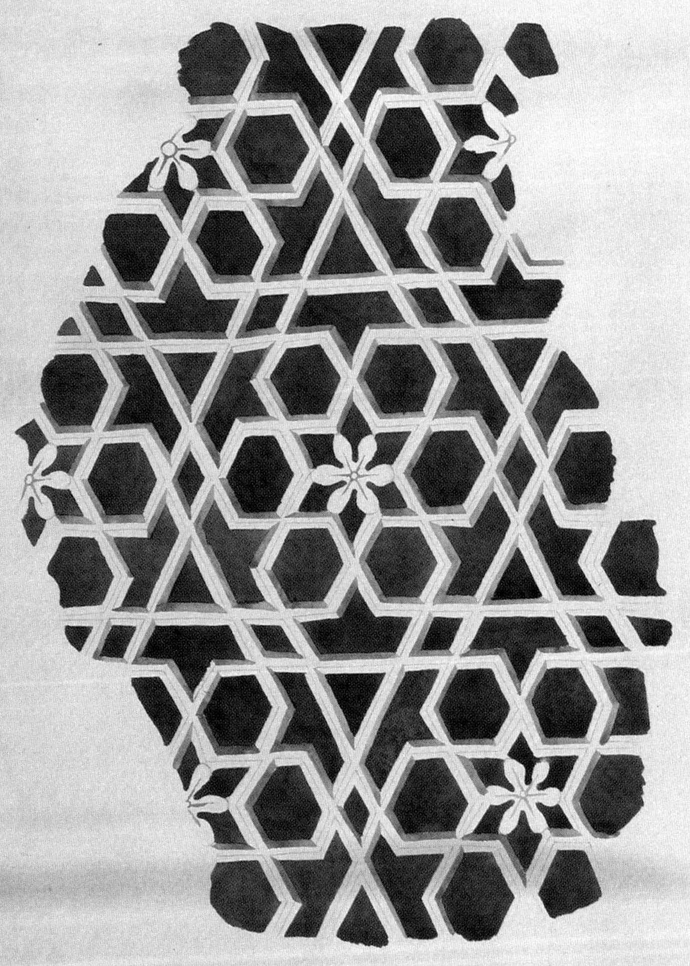

Rubbing from Stone Carvings, Agra District
1052^a 1883.1.5

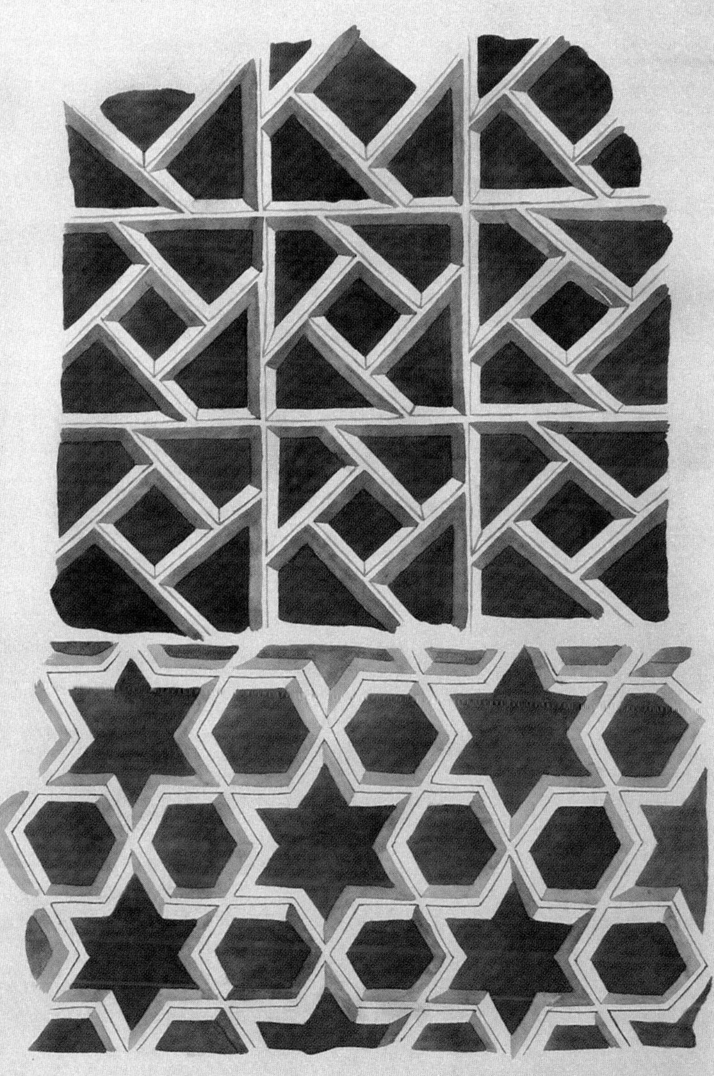

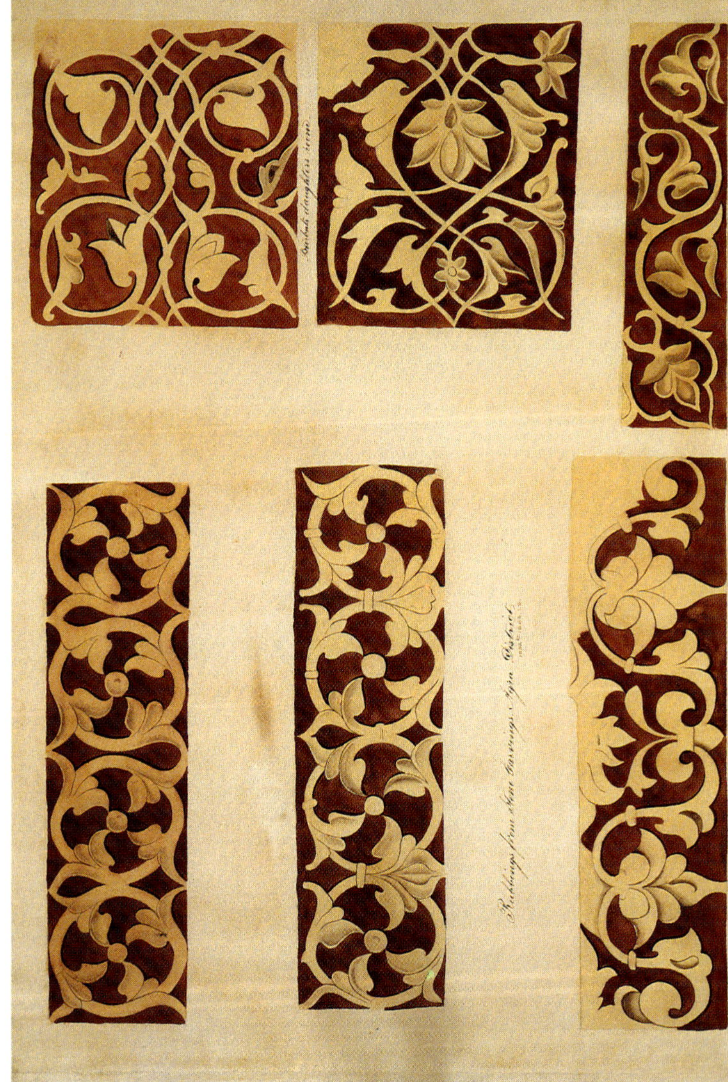

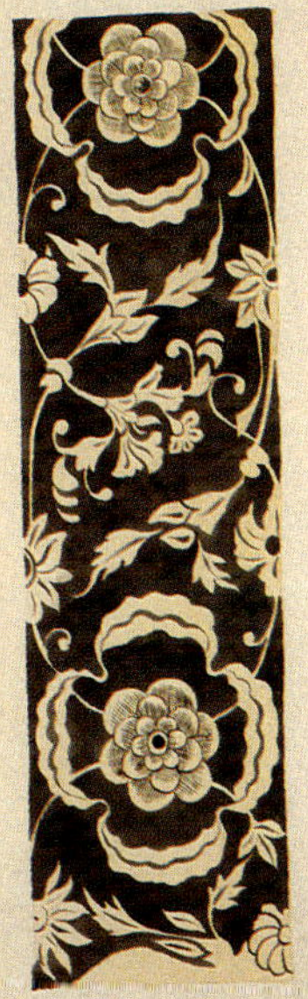

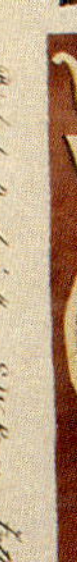

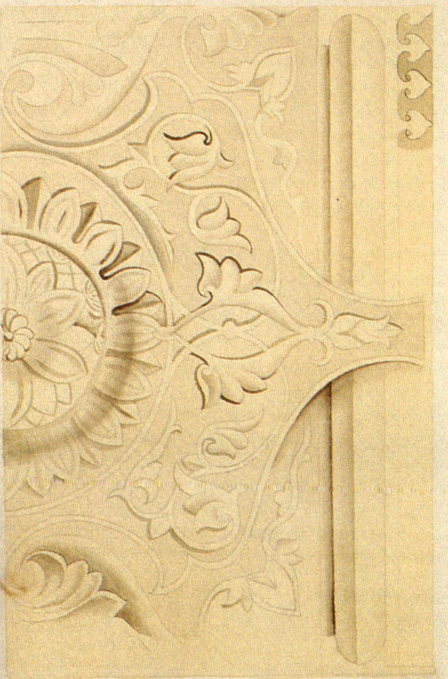

Babul's D. House G.E. Room East doorway base of deen jamb.

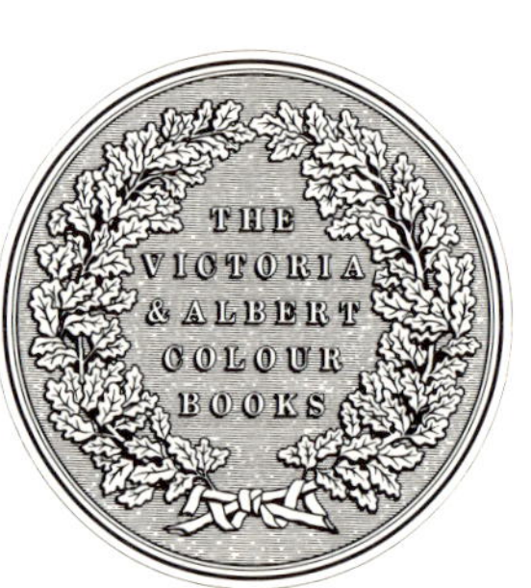
THE
VICTORIA
& ALBERT
COLOUR
BOOKS

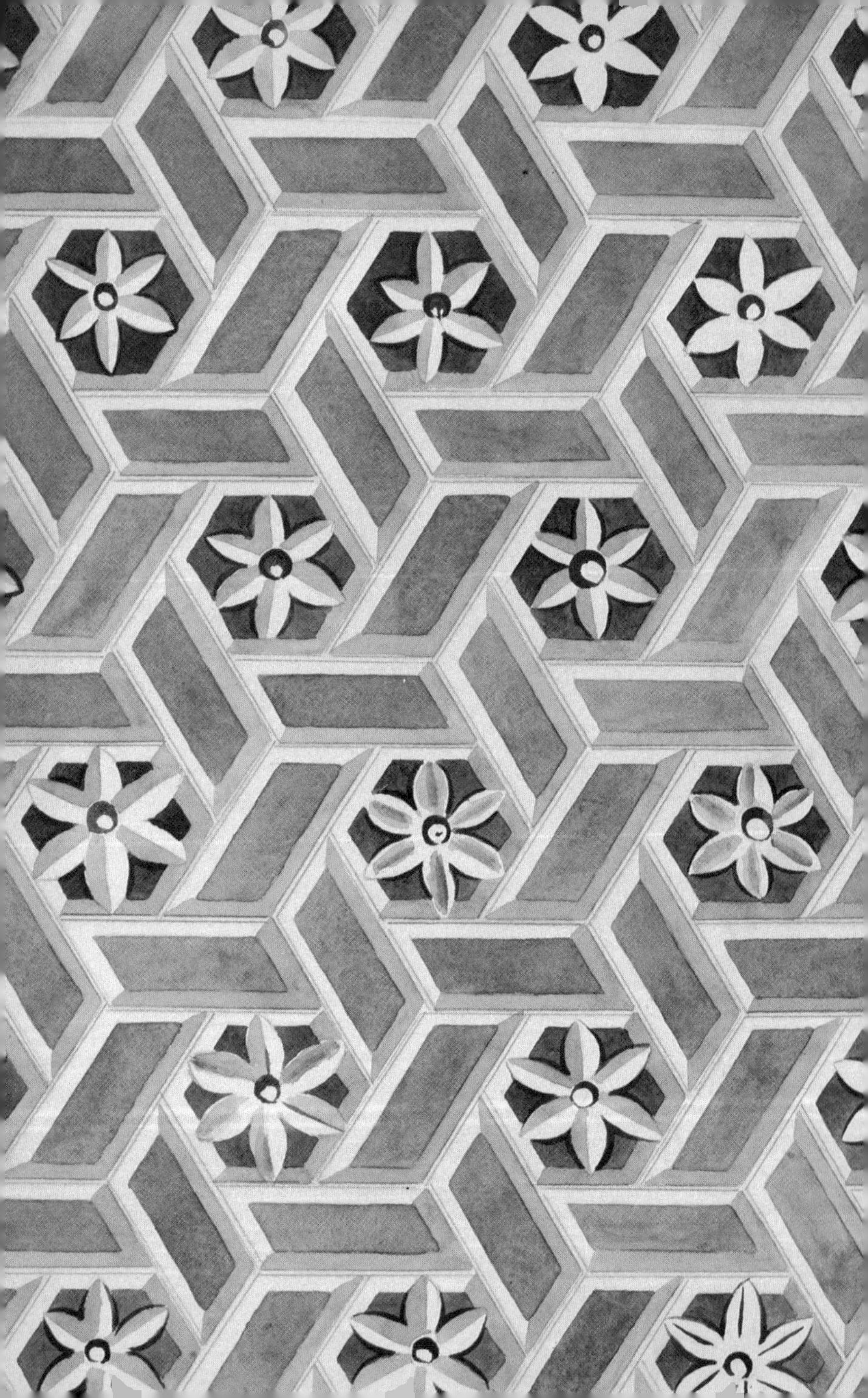